Continent of Fire

Continent of Fire

Poems by

William Considine

© 2022 William Considine. All rights reserved.
This material may not be reproduced in any form, published,
reprinted, recorded, performed, broadcast,
rewritten or redistributed without
the explicit permission of William Considine.
All such actions are strictly prohibited by law.

Cover design by Shay Culligan
Cover image by Denys Argyriou

ISBN: 978-1-63980-176-3

Kelsay Books
502 South 1040 East, A-119
American Fork, Utah 84003
Kelsaybooks.com

For Careen Shannon

Acknowledgments

After the Clouds, the Sun: Continent of Fire, When Here
Brevitas 16: A New Day, Earth Song, Not a Colossus
Brevitas 17: One River, Grain, As If, Bloom
Brevitas 18: City Walk, Fear of Sleep, Rudiments of a Drama, Welcome to Long Island City
Brownstone Poets Anthology 2020: One Plus One
Brownstone Poets Anthology 2021: Unseen
Brownstone Poets Anthology 2022: A Moth
Cover: Bastille
Erasure: Continent of Fire
From Somewhere to Nowhere: Times Square Taxi
Home Planet News 2021: Empedocles at Geysir, Ironworker, Light Fall, Night Essay, Play, Resolution
Live!: Cry Wolf
Poets Reading the News: A Fool Speaks to Power, The Flag Ceremony
POSTporn: Library and Book Sale
POSTstranger: We Migrants
Sensitive Skin: Pale House, Wallace Stevens Loses His Job
Sensitive Skin: Selected Writing 2016–2018: Wallace Stevens Loses His Job
Un Bordado De Voces (An Embroidery of Voices): Gowanus, Sleeping Dragon
White Rabbit: Data Mining, Terminal

I wish to express my appreciation for my colleagues in Brevitas, for the following poetry workshop leaders at The Poetry Project, Bowery Poetry Club, San Miguel Poetry Week, Naropa, Torn Page, Home School, and elsewhere, and for fellow students in their workshops: Priscilla Becker, Anselm Berrigan, Edmund Berrigan, Elizabeth Bishop, Jennifer Clement, Kristine Marie Darling, Will Edmiston, Carter Edwards, James Fenton, Adam Fitzgerald, Dorothy Friedman, Carol Frost, Lisa Jarnot, Jeffrey Levine, Filip Marinovich, Tracie Morris, Elae C. Moss, Harryette Mullen, Elinor Nauen, Hoa Nyugen, Geoffrey G. O'Brien, Kathleen Ossip, Ariana Reines, Luis Alberto Urrea, Anne Waldman, George Wallace, Lewis Warsh and Matvei Yankelevich.

Contents

Earth Song   13

Burnt Soyle

Unseen   17
Plumbing   18
Play   22
Library and Book Sale   24
Rudiments of a Drama   26
The Flag Ceremony   27
We Migrants   34

Metallic Ore

Doctor Doolittle   37
Laura   40
Wallace Stevens Loses His Job   41

The Work of Sulphur

One River   53
Your Face in Sleep   54
It's Time   55
Welcome to Long Island City   56
City Snake   57
Summer   58
Mystery After Hours   59
Terminal   60
Times Square Taxi   62
Night Essay   67
City Walk   68
Grain   69
A Stalwart of Trial Part   70

Veins of Liquid Fire

Pale House	73
Bastille	74
Marcy	75
Dream of a Central States Pension Fund	77
A Fool Speaks to Power	79
My First Oration	80
Not a Colossus	82
As If	83
Data Mining	84
Continent of Fire	85
Darkening Hour	86
Light Fall	87
Cry Wolf	88
Fear of Sleep	89
Sleeping Dragon	90
Our Song	92

By All His Engins

A New Day	95
Gowanus	96
When Here	98
Resolution	99
Our Real Estate	100
A Moth	101
V	102
From the Stars	103
Live as a Poet by Example	104
to Create a New World	104
One Plus One	105
Bloom	106
Sunday, March 15, 2020	107
Together Daily	108

Sunday, March 14, 2021	109
Chasms	110
Ironworker	111
Empedocles at Geysir	112
What a Sun God Sees	113

Earth Song

Earth is river valleys
Restructured as millworks.

Machines feed off barges and long, slow
Trainloads of coal rumbling down nights
Into sleep. Work shift whistles set loose
Crowds of workmen streaming out the gate.

A train of ladle cars tips the brimming
Waste ores, slag, to pour
Molten, white-hot and sparking,
Down a hillside bright in darkness,

Incidental to extraction,
Like our pairings in the off-hours.

Burnt Soyle

Unseen

Today I walked to the ironmaster's shop,
Mender of beds broken—
A deep garage, the sharp dust of cuttings,
The metal tang of copper and iron
And that old smell . . . the odor of Go-Jo solvent,
An oil gel, a salve to wash hands & forearms
Of pipe & grime. Benzene? My madeleine,
A roughed-in doorframe . . .

My father's hands
Glistening in Go-Jo
Scooped from a canister,
Clasped in cleaning,
The dirt sliding away,
And now my hands too,
Turning in the basement.
The furnace and hot water heater
Enclose us; the floor beams cover us.
The pilot light is steady as the threat of hell.

Footfalls overhead, Mom in the kitchen.

What next? Did we talk quietly and laugh
Around the table at dinner,
In that one night, returned from fifty years,
Or did all go wrong again, Dad drive off?

Plumbing

I remember in repair jobs:
>   —stuck, bent nails we have to pry & tug,
>   —knots that rip saw blades,
>   —the usefulness of a crow-bar
>   to rip up floorboards,
>   —a screeching power drill,
>   —and Go-Jo grease to get your hands clean.

>   The trap under the sink
>   is a tough spot, twisting,
>   straining for an angle
>   with a monkey wrench in your face,
>   down on your knees, shoulder, and back.

As a boy, I walked the plank
>   over the moat
onto the foundations of new houses,
dug into the ground in suburbs around 1960.
>   A new lot is a battlefield,
>   raw dirt strewn with debris and
>   heavy equipment.
I scamper on yellow bulldozers.

My dad and I walk through walls
made of lathing and two-by-fours
to rough-in the pipes. We:

>   Drop a
>   plumb
>   line
>   and
>   measure with a folding rule and pencil stub,

Unload from the truck long water pipes
    —slim copper tubing—
and sewer pipe of black iron.

Hold pipe in a vise on a tripod,
measure twice and squeeze
the pipe-cutter, a wrench with a blade.

    Twist and turn, twist and turn,
    exposing bright, unoxidized metal,
    till the loose
            piece

            drops.

    Sort elbow-joints, T-joints, I-joints and valves
            from trays in toolboxes.

    Click wire with a thumb
            across a flint roller
            to set off a spark,
    while easing the valve open on a blowtorch.

Whoosh! Fire bursts out and roars.

    Solder joints and valves onto pipe
        by melting solder like silver to seal the joints
        with a blue-flamed, gasping blowtorch.

Run water pipes as slim twins, always tracing hot from the
water heater along the basement ceiling and up to

kitchen, laundry, bathrooms and powder room.
Hook up the heavy hot water heater and test its fire.

      Push
         big
            bathtubs
               in crates
                  upstairs,
                     cursing
                  the fashion.

Put up air-pressure pipe
        through the roof, steep and scary.

Dig a ditch to the street
and lay pipe
        to reach the main-pipes and tap-in
        to water, sewer and gas lines.

If a toilet or sewer line stops up
—someone dropped something in there—
yank on the plumber's helper
for suction till it pops.

If that doesn't work,
feed a twisting, fundamental snake
        shrieking into the sewer,
thrust, twirl & thrust the snake
 to open clogged pipes. Then

turn on shiny new faucets to see
                    clear
                    water
                    pour
                    and
                    flow.

Play

A little boy
bangs on a metal lamppost
with a bat, heralding
a cooler sunset.

A red rubber ball rolls
toward the street corner
and drops into the storm sewer.
The manhole cover
is too heavy to pry
and lift open.
And we can't play stickball.

Streetlights come on.
The game changes
from rounders to spud
with a volleyball.
Who's "It?"

Run when the ball's thrown high.
Freeze when it's caught
and while it's thrown at you.
I like that game.

Next is hide-and-seek.
"Allee-allee in-free!"
is a call at darkness.

More winners appear
from behind the garage,
hedges and porches,
garbage cans and cars.
Mothers call us home.

In bright electric houses
are homework and TV.

       Parents:
            "Get undressed."
            "Go take a bath."
            "Put on your pajamas."
            "Cut it out in here
            and go to sleep."

Library and Book Sale

The library, the Carnegie Free Library, was up a long walk on a rise. It's grey stone with a tower. Back then, it was black stone, a dark castle keep, all soot from Carnegie's mills down the hill and along the rivers. First, there were the children's books, the Hardy Boys and their chums catching smugglers, Chip Hilton playing all the sports in high school and college, and so many Landmark Books, biography and history, Jules Verne in illustrated editions, then the adult stacks, Hemingway and Faulkner, Robert Frost, Sinclair Lewis, and Upton Sinclair, all free. I persuaded my brothers to walk the long way with me, down our steep hillside, then gradually up and along a ridge a mile lined with houses. I carried piles of books back from Carnegie Library and later married a girl from Library Street.

Then paperbacks bloomed, on revolving wire racks in 5-and-10's, smoke shops and newsstands, cheap and lurid: Bantam Books, Signet, Dell, science fiction in DAW double editions, start one novel from the front, flip it upside down and read the other novel from the other front. J. Edgar Hoover on The Enemy Within, 30 Days to Words of Power, How to Win Friends and Influence People by Dale Carnegie, no relation, right?

My parents bought an encyclopedia from a door-to-door salesman and let me subscribe to the Book of the Month Club: The Rise and Fall of the Third Reich, the Civil War books of Bruce Catton. The Making of the President, 1960, the Collected Plays of Eugene O'Neill. As a club bonus, I got a bridge book, Goren on Bridge, because my aunt was teaching me to play bridge, to be her partner. Then I felt ashamed of the bridge book, my time and my parents' money squandered on a card game. I threw it out and hid it at the bottom of our garbage can, but nothing could be hidden from my parents. I was confronted with the mystery: why did I throw out the bridge book? They turned out not to be hard on me, just said if I didn't want to play bridge anymore, I could tell them.

Then a bookstore appeared by the railroad tracks, in the middle of town, next to a sparsely stocked record store where I'd bought some Motown 45s. Book Sale was the store, with Dianetics and self-help books on tables, surrounded by wall shelves full of paperbacks with the front cover torn off. Torn covers were a cover story, sent back to the distributor, the books' wholesale price refunded by publishers for unsold books, and then the torn-cover books sold through outlets like Book Sale. There I bought Catch-22 in torn cover paperback to devour summer days on a porch swing. Bertrand Russell taught me logic. In one nook were classics, and I found Virgil and the Oresteia in Mentor Classics from New American Library and Shakespeare's plays from Bantam. In another section was the porn, also with covers torn off. Sometimes the clerk barked at me to get away from there; sometimes, he let me buy. One classic had portions like porn: Juvenal's Satires.

One day I heard the clerk tell a friend at the front counter, "Here, you have to see this, it's a big seller, translated from French, you won't believe it. Here, read this part; it's all like that." That was about a new hardcover, in a plain white jacket, kept in a stack at the cashier. I got to it, in time. But more than porn, I craved illicit, cheap, cover-torn classics.

Rudiments of a Drama

Her voice was a needle.
The pain was precise,
Radiating through every nerve,
A life reduced to all awful feelings.

A cloud covered morning
Like an overwhelmed mother.
The view from the cliff was
An ocean churning with rage.

It was already dawn, but
The darkness went on for years.

The Flag Ceremony

This is a story from nearly sixty years ago.
Many kids in those days took part in Scouting.
Little boys belonged in Cub Scouts,
bigger kids in Boy Scouts, and up
to worldly, accomplished Explorers with
canoes, camps, badges, red sashes, and berets.
All got together in Scout Jamborees, like fairs
in the County Park with booths and streamers.
They rode on yellow buses to Camp Aliquippa,
a few hours away in a forest beside a lake.
The hubbub of hundreds of boys rose
from a roar to pure soprano.
The boys ate baked beans and hot dogs
from paper plates in picnic pavilions.
They stuck close to their friends in the crush
of identical uniforms.

                                          On a hill
in one city, there were three Scout troops,
meeting at the public and Catholic schools
and the Methodist church. From downtown,
near the mills along the river, you drove
up a bluff, then over a bridge across
a ravine, then up a long rise lined with
houses with backyards on cinder alleys.
Natural gas was drilled here decades ago.
Trolley tracks still lay in brick avenues,
but busses worked the routes over the hills.

One cub scout pack in Grandview Troop
met in the home of Mrs. Satherton,
the den mother, and other mothers helped her.
We joked and played at her kitchen table.

We made leather coin purses and clay things.
We partied with balloons using helium.
We walked entranced around dinosaur bones
in the museum in Pittsburgh.

At the ballpark, we cheered Roberto Clemente
when he threw from deep right field
straight home on one hop to nail a runner,
and the ballpark hummed with murmuring awe.

Mrs. Satherton entertained us
for two years, and that was enough.
Now that the boys were a little older, a man
would be good as a Scout Leader, all agreed.
But the men of the town worked hard in heat,
made steel in mills beside the winding rivers.
Their leisure interests were remote
from the woodlore of Scouting. Men hung out
in bars. Hiking was not done. A hunting trip
might involve a cabin and whiskey.

Then a volunteer came forward. Mr. Slade
was new in town and worked in an office.
He was a hunter and would take the boys
into the woods. His son Ted would join the pack
and get more involved in his new hometown.
Ted was a gentle giant, mild and shy.
He was a near neighbor, and we played.
He had a lively interest in frogs.
I'd been in their home and met timid Mrs. Slade,

fussing at the stove. She said I should leave
before Ted's father got home. We went
out front to play. He came home and
Ted got anxious, watching the windows.

Soon he had to rush inside. He said
his father had gestured at a window,
and he ran. The story he later shared:
his father often beat him with a belt
and punished his mother that way, too,
for all her shortcomings.

                                         But it all
happened so fast. Mr. Slade was the leader
of our pack by consent of the parents.
I could tell no one about the belt.
I had been paddled often enough.
And I knew another boy whose father
used the belt on him and his brother.
I accepted that Mr. Slade was our new leader,
but I was afraid—and I liked Scouting,
its teaching new ways to play, new skills,
its big magazine, "Boys Life," its handbook
of splints and knots, lifesaving first-aid tips,
Indian lore and songs of the forest.

Word of the next meeting came
on the phone to our fathers.
Eight boys of different sizes met
in the park after school, late afternoon,
in a grassy field near the foot of the hill.

We wore our uniform blue shirts
with jeans or uniform blue pants.
Mr. Slade said he would teach us
discipline and proper respect for the flag.
We would learn today to fold the flag.
He pulled it from a box on a picnic table
as we stood in two ranks. Look, he said.
Our country's flag was in his hands.

He opened it and told us what we knew
already about the stars and stripes.
He told us to stop fidgeting.
You must never throw a flag away,
he said. What do you do with a worn-out flag?
Ted knew. You burn it. Right, you burn the flag.
What do you do at sunset?
At sunset, you pull it down and fold it.

He put us in teams to practice folding the flag.
He taught too fast, and no one got it right.
We talked among ourselves how to do it.
He told us to be quiet and watch, then
taught us two at a time and sent the others
ten yards away to wait and be quiet.
By then, the Cub Scouts were unhappy,
standing in silence in the park with nothing
to do in the tension of displeasing
our Scout Leader. I muttered, "This is fun,"
and Mr. Slade yelled at me for talking
while other boys were learning to fold the flag.
Mr. Slade gave me another chance, tried
to be patient as I practiced in turn.

Next, we would learn a flag ceremony
with candles. He had mimeograph copies
of the text of a ceremony,
copies that smelled lusciously of ink.
It involved four corners of flag and country,
four winds, and a square of
four boys, holding candles and
stepping and reciting like altar boys.
We practiced our steps and took too long.

It was getting dark, but all the better
for the upcoming lit candle effect.
Okay, we'd have to read our lines this time.
We split into two groups of four.
My group would go first, and the others
should get out of the way and watch.
Mr. Slade produced the candles. He lit one.
A brisk evening wind, in a horizontal
flare of flame and wisp of smoke, blew it out.
He tried to light candles in our cupped hands,
again and again, but the wind was steady.

Mr. Slade lit a candle in the lee of his body
and big hands and passed it to a boy.
The wind slackened as if to his will.
He lit and passed four candles.
We four boys approached the center solemnly,
holding paper, flag, and flickering
candles in the darkening field.
We stumbled through the opening lines
in piping young voices. At once,

the wind flared and blew out our candles.
I snickered at the inevitable,
the folly of candles in the wind
snickered out of nervousness.

Mr. Slade yelled. "How dare you! It's not funny!
That's disrespect for the flag—disrespect
for veterans! Your father will hear about this!
We'll do it again. This time, do it right!"
Mr. Slade decided not to light the candles.
We boys read from the text, moved as directed,
and watched the other group do the same.

It was dark, and Mr. Slade drove a few boys home
in his car. I walked home alone.
I had failed in Scouting.
My father would be mad, but
it was not disrespect for the flag.
Mr. Slade used the flag to boss people around.
This impulsive thought was too extreme to say
to boys who just wanted to get away.

At home, I said the Scout meeting was boring
and not thought out. Mr. Slade was too bossy,
and I didn't like Scouting anymore.
Soon the phone rang, and my mother answered.
It was Mr. Slade, asking to speak with my dad.

I watched Dad, still in his plumbing clothes—
green shirt and pants, sturdy shoes—take the phone.
He looked at the ceiling, saying, "Uh-huh, uh-huh."

Soon he said, "Well, I'll talk to him about it.
Good-bye," and hung up. As I watched nervously,
he laughed. "What happened to you today?"
A little way later, Dad called Mr. Slade.
"I've decided to let my son quit your Scout group,"
he said. "Well, nothing happened to criticize
him for. There was no disrespect for the flag.
We don't want to get into those kinds of discussions."

The pack continued, reduced in number.
Later, it developed that Mr. Slade belonged
to a political group that aimed to take over
Scouting, the John Birch Society.
It had bad press then, and for all his activities
in PTA, too, Mr. Slade was a solitary figure
known as an extremist. The times have changed.

We Migrants

I migrated from a mill town,
first to college, then New York,
never planning to return.

As the oldest of three boys,
I separated from my brothers,
left them, got out of town
and a troubled family.

Not that I'd been
a protective older brother,
but leaving clinched it –
I was not.

Later, both my brothers migrated
West, to different states.
We were dispersed.

Rare phone calls
or, later, text message
holiday greetings
passed between us.

Metallic Ore

Doctor Doolittle

Astronomer:

I sit slouched on a steamer trunk
waiting for the awful departure, Hilda
leaving across the ocean
to Europe to see that cad, the feral Ezra.
They were engaged! No more.
Still, she's going weeks away, my darling
girl, nervous and determined, bold
and so sensitive. The poetic
it seems has taken hold,
a form of intellect, of study
under the moon and its charges
dangerously close to astrology,
uncertain, fickle, poor.
Still, she's excited, lively.

Bill is here to see her off,
a doctor now, a much better
man, but not wild
enough for her, and she's too much
for him. Married in New Jersey
or out talking late into the bright night
in Paris? We know where our Hilda goes.
We gave her the best education,
though hard for her to swallow.
She took her medicine and thrived
with long limbs stretching.
She'll surpass her quiet father,
love sitting stacked on the luggage
to help her leave.

How glum I must look, to lose my daughter
to Europe and the peacock Ezra.
What enthusiasms and dramas!
I can't stop her from going. Art
is what's important to her. She's strong
enough for Paris and poems.

A giant star pulls me in by its mass
of atom gasses to flare and burn.
This is my night in flames.

The stars:

Searching local skies,
you can't imagine what
your daughter will endure.
And your son—you left him home.
Europe will call him too,
standing straight in duty's uniform.
Constellations of ignorance ignite skies,
artillery barrages
to drive men mad to go over
into machine guns.
When the enemy is in your trench,
he's trapped.
Time has trapped your boy.
That's the loss that will break you, Doctor,
with Hilda helpless and far.

Astronomer:

The stars only seem silent.
Their fiery din does not reach us.
The moon follows her.

Laura

*"The Muse is a deity, but she is also a woman . . .
Laura Riding has spoken on her behalf in . . .
memorable lines."*
—Robert Graves

Robert says his girlfriend, Laura, may be
The living avatar of the goddess
Ruling the world throughout archaic time.
He exclaims her name at climax of his book.

Laura says his goddess claims lack rigor,
And it's really embarrassing for Bob
To bring Laura into it, to stand for
His hopes as a thinker and poet. Plus,

Both lovers dropped away out the windows.
Laura finds a steadier guy. They're joined
In academic endeavors too. With him,
She finds the fine demands of poetry

For proud displays for fellow craft-workers
Always give rise to lies, or if that's too much,
Obscure more than intimate what is true.
She sets aside her art to write plainly.

Though silver bells and tinsel are gleaming,
In sacred jest, the art's only seeming.

Wallace Stevens Loses His Job

Moment in flux: Tuesday, February 8, 1916.
Place in passing: 55 Liberty Street, Manhattan,
    New York City:
a new tower, the Liberty Nassau Building,
Liberty Tower, first called the Bryant Building for
William Cullen Bryant, poet of "Thanatopsis" and the
    Green River,
Editor, New York Evening Post
in the prior building on the site, just below Printers Row,
    Park Row.

Liberty Street: formerly Crown Street,
three blocks north of Wall: Pine, Cedar, Liberty.
Next North: Maiden Lane, ambiguous name
for the course of a brook and a path beside it,
its vale still curving and descending to the East River.

In 1916, six years old, the Bryant Building
re-named Liberty Tower
holds many small offices for
lawyers, stockbrokers, and financiers, including
former President Theodore Roosevelt.

One such enterprise is New England Equitable Insurance
    Company
(or perhaps the Equitable Assurance Company of
    St. Louis, Missouri).
It sells fidelity and surety bonds, and a vice president
in the New York office is thirty-six years old,
married and on his own time sometimes writes poems,
one Wallace Stevens, Harvard man, lawyer.
His "Sunday Morning" was published recently

in Harriet Monroe's magazine from Chicago,
Poetry,
       chopped short,
              stanzas rearranged.

              But down to business:
Otis elevators allow concentration in small areas
like this Financial District, mean economies
in transportation costs and communication of
sales ideas, people interfacing like microchips do now,
such fast facial exchanges expressed within tall buildings in
clusters, motherboards sparking
with energy. Everyone is building
—though this year has been weaker—
so the market for surety bonds
to guarantee completion of construction is thriving.
Dealings must be down to earth into bedrock,
people assessed, finances assessed, defaults stark
in measure and remedies structured in terms precisely.

It had been a rough haul for Stevens
through New York Law School right here
and several firms and businesses on these few blocks:

       interning with W.G. Peckham, attorney at law,
a Harvard connection, an *Advocate* alum, and friend,
    then Eaton and Lewis, the leading firm in insurance,
                   then months unemployed,
         then Eustis and Foster,
                or Fidelity and Deposit,
     then partners with Lyman Ward
     with few clients, then

                  American Bonding Company,
    now two years here.

Now things were looking up like people to skyscrapers
out of Chicago and the Beaux-Arts tradition.

But—Europe is at war, insane.
This week: Guns Open Attacks—Saloniki Line and
Pound Strategic Points from Somme River to
Lorraine—Big Assault in West Expected.
Settlement Near on Lusitania—
Wrest Submarine Weapon from Germany.
Germany, Self-Fed, Defies Her Enemies.
Fear of Rupture—America Has Sided with Allies –
Kaiser's Son Wounded Again.

Locus on earth: center of capital.
55 Liberty Street: corner of Nassau:
handsome, slim tower,
white terra cotta coated steel cage construction,
caissons forced deep into rock foundation.
Its style is Neo-Gothic—churchy like the resonance of
poetry, all immanence and epiphany—
with humorous touches:
Grinning, agile alligators grasp and climb the front—
biting at flora from fabled Florida.
A bay window, two stories high, juts out over
a single bronze and glass revolving door.
(Where's the door, they ask in studio; here, it's clear.)

Young Mr. Stevens is at work in a three-piece suit
somewhere in what is now a luxury co-op apartment
in Liberty Tower, along an exterior wall, in a manager's office,
double-windowed, with a half-glass door and dividing wall
to let light pass into the central staff area,
when word comes from Boston (or St. Louis)
by earpiece on a two-piece phone,
in his office or next door in Ed Southworth's,
that the New York office is closing. Now.
Shut it down; it's over.
People will get paid through today (or so, actual terms
    not known.)
You can put files in order for auditors and attorneys,
answering questions, and then afraid you're out.

Not entirely a surprise:
The Board had fired the company President last month.
Rumors were the books were troubling
at New England when they bought St. Louis.
The money isn't there, theft with a pen
at headquarters exposed by the market weakening,
and insufficient inflow to cover the risks taken.
Though the business looked promising, its proceeds are sunk
into paper transactions, notes below water, cash gone.

Ed Southworth and Wallace Stevens call the staff
together and tell them they're all let go, to anger, tears,
dismay. Voices are raised, outrage.
Men and women lose their legs and sit despondently.
Not leaving without my money, they say,
but leave with promises.

In early evening, Stevens exits an elevator into
the marble lobby, past a bust of William Cullen Bryant,
looking up to tall, narrow windows—a sacristy of suits—
and spirals in the sole revolving door
    through bronze décor.
He looks left to 84 William Street, red brick
    rounding the bend
where Maiden Lane meets Liberty and William,
where he used to work for American Bonding Company
of Baltimore on the seventh floor,
assistant manager, two blocks, two years ago.

                        Could he go back there?
But all his crowd have moved on. (Now it's a dorm for
New School and Pace students, no, now it's
been converted behind scaffolds into luxury condos.)
He has to reinvent himself again, like a line in a poem.

He looks down narrow Nassau into Broad Street
at Federal Hall, the stone Greek temple
of the site of Washington's inauguration.
In 1916, it's the U. S. Sub-Treasury Building,
where many tons of gold are stored.
(Now, that gold and more is stored just left of him,
under the palazzo of the Federal Reserve.)
With Broad Street curving, in the view straight ahead,
the perspectival focus of the narrow Nassau way
is the front of the New York Stock Exchange,
a large, columned temple extruding from a wall.

This block at Liberty is the swell of a knoll, a high point
descending three ways to water,
to rivers, harbor, and turbulent, grasping sea.

Wallace Stevens turns right in the dark and heads west
with the evening rush hour crowds along Liberty Street
past the New York Chamber of Commerce Building,
more solemn columns and large round portholes
alluding to the sea trade
(now home to The Central Bank of China, Taipei).

As we walk west with the unemployed, ahead
is the Turkish delight of the Singer Building,
cupola on high, another wild weed coursing with
elevator juice, and jammed right beside it,
the lopsided City Investing Building.
Singer makes tabletop machines,
so many men and women doing piecework
at machines in loft buildings uptown
in the Lower East Side, and
in the back room of a dimly lit candy store,
behind a curtain into the parlor
(the main enterprise in the ground floor
storefront apartment is sewing)
and out to prairies and cities,
sewing to clothe the people.

To the left, seen above older buildings
for banking and paper transfers,
is the most massive office building of all,
the Equitable Building,

newly completed as a rental property
filling all its city block thirty times over,
forty stories straight up,
1.2 million square feet, room enough
for 16,000 workers, men in authority
and women assisting.
In daytime it casts shadows over all
the surroundings, darkening the district.

Just south of Pine, the American Surety Company
has its own substantial building too,
fronted with militant, mature women, Greek goddesses.
American Surety—his book of business was good, but
lawyers in that building will succeed to it.
(Now it's the Bank of Tokyo Building.)

> *Who do I know there?*
> *Too much movement on my resume.*
> *Now fresh from a failed company.*

What a building boom this is, so much surety work.
Left down Broadway are twin Trinity Buildings,
Tall and dripping with swag,
then the old graveyard, bare in winter, and
the brownstone, steepled church.
Just south of Rector Street,
US Steel rules regions and states
from the Empire Building,
eldest of the Trinity triplets.

Standard Oil is further down,
and Shippers Row will grow from the sea,
white, beige, ivory buildings:
U.S. Lines—Panama Pacific will build at 1 Broadway,
Cunard Lines may build; Adams Express has built
and American Express will build new headquarters
in front of their warehouse, all this is in the works.

Stevens turns right on Broadway, north
into the diamond district, over the clock in the sidewalk.
He's thinking about work and ruin.
Across Broadway is a construction site to be
    headquarters for
the American Telephone and Telegraph Company,
white columns of grandeur and authority all over it.

Further north for looking up is the Woolworth Building,
newly completed, tallest in the world,
twice the height of Liberty Tower,
with more Gothic drapery.
So much around is Greek or Gothic, reason and faith.
Woolworth built with bargains in five & ten-cent stores,
women attentive behind counters and selling goods to
    women.
Singer and Woolworth are selling goods to go
with buildings in boom times.

Stevens sees the column cake of the Post Office ahead,
but turns right onto Fulton Street.
(Fulton's steamship worked these rivers,
Fulton lies buried in Trinity Yard.)

He thought he'd walk home to plan what he'd say
to Elsie, but it's cold.
Among peddlers of pamphlets, books, and belts,
he walks slowly down the stairs
into the subway station at Fulton, East Side IRT,
the only subway downtown.
The West Side IRT is under construction downtown.
The BMT is under construction.
The subway tunnel east to Brooklyn is under
    construction.
Steel rails are laid by hand underground and underwater
in tubes, like cables of fiber optics.
He'll ride to 23rd Street and walk west to Elsie on
    West 21st Street,
across from the seminary, home to start over again.

> *I'll call Jim Kearney in the morning. He's key.*
> *Not Collins Lee.*
> *Jim knows my work. He knows I'm clean.*
> *But Jim prefers Ed Southworth to me . . .*
> *Hartford could use a strong team.*
> *Call Jim in the morning. We'll see.*

The Work of Sulphur

One River

One river's a fiord.
One river's an estuary.

Both swell with the ocean
and flow upstream.

The sea reaches to embrace
an island within them.

Waters caress, waters
pass by and return.

Sway, stay,
sway, stay.

Your Face in Sleep

Your face in sleep is self-absorbed in grace,
As constellations flow among the stars,
      In featureless repose that forms all space.

Softer than a dream of flesh, your face
Among the archetypes still flows
      In dim abandon.

What wild wine drama's only trace
      Is smoothed relief?
      What mythos dreams this ease?

It's Time

Otherwise, the short night lets our clinging
Hours vary with sporadic embraces.
We drowse forgetful side by side and sprawl
Among each other's lazy, hot limbs.

In time the air implacably brightens.
Pigeons coo through this last night's departure.
Dressing, you tug and turn in earthy
Silhouette. You stare from the shadows and

Leap into your stockings like a rabbit.
Your face is bloated with squelched tears. I can
Not imagine you gone. How could our room
Hold emptiness of your size and fervor?

Welcome to Long Island City

Sparsely populated warehouse, garage
and workshop landscape, low and packed tight . . .
A rare row of three old wood-frame houses,
freestanding, with high stairs to the front doors . . .

"Why do you think your garden is so lush?"
said a friendly native to a new tenant
in one house. The flowers were startlingly
tall and full, now that he mentioned it.

"Ships unloading sugar at the Pepsi plant
—with that huge neon sign at the river,
directly across from the UN Building?—
"smuggled drugs too, for the French Connection.

"Back then, you'd hear gunshots in the night.
It's said bodies are buried in your backyard."

City Snake

Structural rods are banded, rust-brown shocks,
        hundreds, coiled, entwined, bent,
        emerging from the edges of cement
in hideous rows. Massive blocks
        of smashed buildings fell at the river
in out-of-place piles, like glacial rocks
        where snakes stretch in the sun's shiver.

Sun on a slab yourself and see the city
        across the wide merging of a creek
        and a river at noon. The pretty
confluence of slow, slow waters gleams
        everywhere. Soon your eyes will seek
beneath for fish darting in timbers. It seems
        your gaze finds life within what's gritty.

Summer

Long rest
a retrograde season
sleeping late in drowsy air
of fine yellow pollen

Shaken
rumbling of heavy trucks
and word talk forming
into work,
awake

        The night:
loud, hot drinking
in a purple-lit basement bar
performing to stay alive,
alive.

        What's this—
more poetry?

Dark bars are not the best places.
A dull cocaine addict puts
her hands in my pockets
looking for dollars.

All I do is go to church
to hear new poems
and I've been robbed in
a bar, like no innocent.

        Yes, ask Sappho
how she feels about thighs.

Mystery After Hours

Someone had told me of a new after-hours bar
in the neighborhood. Returning late
one night from Lower East Side
arts events and gatherings,
by subway to the Old Courthouse Square,
riled up, still awake, energy
unlimited and driving me,
demanding more, down empty streets,
I found the covert bar.
The few men there looked at me warily
and said little. Well, one thing.

Someone whispered the place was run
by the local police precinct captain,
and it seemed to be so because
he came in, in uniform, made
the rounds and spoke with me briefly,
asking who I was and why I'd come.
I decided these waterfront
night waters were far too deep
for a tourist, finished my beer
and never dared,
never wanted to go back.

Terminal

New York harbor was great
enough for the US Army,
setting off to take Europe
from the altar of a three-faced God
to kill Germans gone mad.

The most massive concrete
building on earth,
unheated, waterless, sky-lit,
bare, for trains of armor
reaching into the sea . . .

Pigeons flock in the broken
sky-chamber.
Here is the tomb,
broken open.

Call this a concrete cathedral,
built to conquer Rome.
In the great hall of Atreus:
eighteen feet of loading
platform for a stage:
the tomb of Agamemnon:
here is the scene of our sacrifice.

"The warlord is dead!"
I make children cry.
I slit their throats
at high concrete columns of
the troops of goodbye, my love.

Turning over earth
in the railroad tracks, I bury
far-fallen glass with the paint of
our blood performance.

Times Square Taxi

West 42nd Street between 7th and 8th Avenues was so
desolate and disreputable, it wasn't even our address.
The official address was 221 W. 41st Street.
That door led to a long hallway north
to the lobby off 42nd Street. (The hallway's still there,
inside the McDonalds that's there now, crowded, narrow, lined
with a shelf for your coke and fries.)

Just a few years earlier, the simple four-story box
on the southwest corner of 7th and 42nd had been the site
of an artists' occupation, guerilla art,
taking over an empty building
to cram it full of art and people, the Times Square Show.
Now the site housed a hotel, a porn shop, and a diner.

The hotel, of course, was for whores and johns
and the pimp who came by for his money, and
a woman from work meeting her boyfriend at lunch hour.
The porn shop was a small black box of nastiness.
The diner had a good bowl of rice and black beans,
cheap, nourishing, and fast, but
the place was open to street life: poverty, insanity, anger.
It was cheap for bustling, turn-over trade, no place to
    linger.

The next establishment along the south side
of West 42nd Street, west of Times Square,
past the newsstand and subway entrance was
a wide-open pizza shop in what was once a theater lobby,
with two counters in a V opening onto the sidewalk.

There, I saw a young pizza counter worker
in white food industry clothes, shouting in rage, pull out
a baseball bat and chase a man down the street.

The block had been deserted by a devastated industry,
or rather a shift in the entertainment business
to other products with better returns.
The big theaters filled with dancing choruses and song
were silent now and left behind to decay
by the rapid advance of radio, movies, and television.
A few theaters still showed older films to
a tiny audience scattered among a thousand seats.

On the street, "You broke my bottle" was the roughest con.
A big guy, his arms and shoulders bare in a white
   undershirt,
would be fumbling on the sidewalk to light a cigarette.
As you passed, giving plenty of room, he'd lurch into you
and ask you to hold this for a second:
a quart bottle of beer. It fell
to the sidewalk, maybe breaking, beer splashing, and
now the guy was angry and confrontational—
"You broke my bottle!"—and he wanted you to pay for it,
straight out extortion on the sidewalk.
"It cost ten dollars."
He wanted money, and it was hard to walk away.
He was poor, unsteady, strong, and angry.

A man and a woman, a happy couple, laughing, embracing,
focused on each other, in fact
raucous, drunk and loud, come heedless and fast.

They suddenly walk right into you and
SQUIRT you
—the woman has a mustard squeeze bottle!
Mustard on your clothes!—
They're so apologetic and pathetic.
They paw at you and try to wipe the mustard off
your clothes, smearing it, mortified,
and you push them off and wave them away
as they apologize loudly. Later you find your wallet gone.

But the sale of crack cocaine,
at the height of the epidemic in the late Eighties,
was the main business on the sidewalks.
The dealing was run from midblock, in front of
the Candler Building, our building,
where we City government workers labored daily.
The Candler Building had been the headquarters
for the Coca-Cola Company. A block to its west
was the pale blue, modern McGraw Hill Building.
Across 43rd was the mass of the Times Building.
Those were the only tall buildings.

Crack or whatever else
(I remember heroin junkies nodding, swaying stiffly,
barely upright on the sidewalk near the newsstand)
was sold under what's now the canopy for McDonald's,
just out the front door below our offices.
There was a mailbox at the curb that seemed to serve
as the head drug dealer's throne.
He could lean on the mailbox or sit on it. Around him
was a cloud of colleagues in atomic stasis or rotation
in a royal court's rituals of watchfulness and readiness.

I had an office on the third floor, overlooking the front.
The police sent a uniformed officer into my office
to watch and report on the street activity.
Crouching on the floor and peering over the low sill,
he described into his walkie-talkie the sales operations as
they took place below, drugs being passed and money
changing hands in separate transactions
on different sides of 42nd Street. Pay him, go there, pick up.
Some buyers went around the corners
onto 41st Street to smoke crack right away.

As a group, they were poor and worn, prematurely aged,
often ragged and dirty, sometimes bruised.
They gathered behind the long-emptied theater east of
our back door,
under its fire escape and sat on an old exit's few steps,
to light up their crack pipes.

West 41st Street was a major thoroughfare for crowds
of pedestrians twice daily. Commuters passed from and to
the Port Authority Bus Terminal on Eighth Avenue.
They filled the street, a parade at rush hour,
a few cars proceeding slowly among them.

Concerned what needy people high on drugs might do
to the people passing back and forth on West 41st Street,
we joined with the few other businesses on the block
—a theater, a bar—to form a Block Association and
chipped-in funds to hire a security service
with several German shepherd dogs.

They were kenneled in the basement of our building and
brought out at mid-day and again before the evening rush,
just one or two at a time on leashes, to walk the block.
Seeing them soon drove away the young people
who had sadly become addicted to the new drug crack,
but the dogs howled at night in the basement in misery
and we had to end it.

Night Essay

A tired man struggles
to hint about the death
of poems in his time
after work and dinner.

The effort produces signs
of exhaustion,
with irony about self
and other depletions.

You, Reader of Puzzles,
quickly catch a rare
breath of resolve.
That's an aesthetic pleasure.

The challenge of recording
one's work in a logbook
avoids the central tendency
to start talking politics.

When the art of government
is the Lie,
embarrassed by my rage,
I fulfill my repression.

A nightmare man,
wrapped around a skeleton, sinks
into shadowed grounds.

Above a seminary's steep roofs,
full summer boughs swirl
with the wind, shushing.

City Walk

As if the city were an alien
place made of cement,
we stroll unyielding ground,
through constant shadows

of wall-to-wall structures.
Idling anxiety whirrs
at the pace of our companion
tons of hurtling traffic.

Where disjunction
shakes a sidewalk
with such spatial relations,
what are free associations?

Grain

Once seen, always a landmark:
tall, grimy concrete grain elevators
of The Port Authority of New York
high over green ballfields, sole in the sky.
Seabirds glide
beside the wave rounded silos,
over still waters, a finger inlet
of Erie Basin, Red Hook, Brooklyn.

Driving through downtown Buffalo
onto the high freeway,
first in the corner of an eye,
head-turning while driving fast
in traffic, I see
lakefront grain elevators massed
on the edge of pale blue, placid Lake Erie.

A Stalwart of Trial Part

The older gentleman in computer training
tries using the mouse as a remote,
picks it up and points at the screen,
clicking emphatically.

God bless him; he can't type either.
All his life, women would type for him.

A stalwart of Trial Part in Kings and Queens Counties,
steady on his feet, wooer and winner
of jurors, well-remembered for kindness
to young attorneys thrown into court,

now grizzled and graybeards, still active
and earning well into his eighties,
at deskwork presiding and deciding
(though hearing loss excuses some confusions).

He still dictates through a Dictaphone.
That's the machine at his workstation.

. . . Until the day the typist calls
to say she can't follow the tape. She says
he has to hear the tape himself and returns it.
Delay! Fuss! In due course, he presses, Play

to hear the horror of his deep voice going off
wandering, thick and vague through
trolleys and kitchens to mom's pancakes
in puzzled musing what the case takes.

Veins of Liquid Fire

Pale House

You should not enter the House of the Inquisitor.
Its pale stone, floral-ornamented frontage wall
Is locked. It was built in 1780, when this town

Was larger than any in your country, a depot
Serving slave silver mines, two days distant,
That fed a cruel empire's grind and grasping.

Small rooms remain in the basement, it's said.
You've seen the implements of torture, the head screw.
Indigenous peoples clung to traces of their old faiths.

The prior house on your lot was bewitched, you learn.
Witches live along this street. They thrive beside
The stream like willows and will so long as water lasts.

Bastille

Start with Laura of the love
sonnets. She gave birth to de Sade.
He incited the poor crowd
from a tower cell above
the high-walled, barren Bastille, called
down, "Citizens, save us!
They're torturing us!"
He was taken in the night
to a new madhouse. Storming and fall
the next day meant nothing.
The mob in his cell in fright
and anger at writing tore
up his plays. The Terror
soon sentenced him to die.
He spied
        down captive
     on the guillotine
   festival of
 the free.

Marcy

Marcy from Troy was a Bucktail,
Opposed to the Erie Canal,
New York Governor, US Senator,
Secretary of War for the Mexican War,
Collapsed from the strain of
Supplying two armies in desert aggression.

Marcy was a Hunker, a Soft, a Doughface
(Doe face) Democrat, open
To bargaining with Barnburners
Who opposed slavery,
But a Unionist, loyal to the solid South
Leadership of the Democracy,
The Slave Power, a massive wealth.
Representing New York
And its bankers and merchants,
He served the Fire-eaters:
> *Slavery's in the Constitution.*
> *Slave-owner votes are multiplied.*
> *It's basic to our Union deal.*

Marcy, betrayed by rivals and Hards,
Lost his last bid for the Presidency
To "a handsome alcoholic with fewer enemies,"
Then served as Secretary of State,
For he was a statesman and Unionist.
Marcy made the Gadsden Purchase
Of land for a southern railway to California.
Marcy pressed Spain to sell us
Cuba and its slaves.
Marcy approved private army
Filibuster gang expeditions invading

Mexico and Nicaragua.

Marcy worked so hard
To spread slavery south and west,
To preserve the Union.

Marcy dying saw the confusion of
Fusion parties coming on fast:
Know-Nothing, Free Soil, Republican.
Soon Unionist meant the opposite,
As the Fire-eaters seceded and attacked.

Dream of a Central States Pension Fund

High wheelers, big rigs, semis, 18-wheelers
Pull freight, haul massive freight,
Puncture, burn, shred & shed
Rubber tire tubing, strewn along shoulders
Of Interstate highways & twisting turnpike,
Mile after roaring mile.

Days and ill-lit nights before
Concrete set in Jersey barriers
Reduced the terrible head-ons,
Strong-arm men with bullets and bats set upon
Workingmen dispersed in commerce.
 I won't name names.

Drivers entered tunnels of unspeakable
Exposure to assault. Each switched on
High beam headlights of the Elect.
They stayed in lane, voted for the union slate.
The union won them all a pension.
The pension fund was found money.

Flatlands of the Central States
Promised bounty in earthbound
Toil, yielding corn if water,
If winds are mild, cold abated,
The land was taken & tried,
Soil & seasons of mere grasslands.

Need is so great & time driven.
Uphill grades of mountains-crossing
Need pulling power. Amphetamines keep up.
Keep up. This energy speeds, will hurtle—
The new contract, next election.

Pension fund money fuels
Desert capital, dammed oasis,
Casinos to replace Havana:
Las Vegas!

A Fool Speaks to Power

If you want real power, nuncle,
Bring back crime. Start by claiming
There's a terrible crime wave, whatever.
Make poor migrants criminals
In hiding, unable to turn to the police.
Make up new crimes, enforce the obsolete.
Marijuana, nuncle—such a haze so
Fraught for paranoia—Lock them up!
To be king, you must have prisoners.
Disrupt whole communities,
Charge and ruin them, one by one.
A huge population in private prisons—
Did you know you can own a prison in America?
I heard last night of a guy
Who owns a chain of women's prisons.
They can work for a dollar a day,
Pure profit on prison labor,
Exempt from the constitution's ban on slavery.
They're off the streets and cannot vote.
Their communities are yours, reduced.
That will keep them weak enough
To be subjects of a bitter fool, nuncle,
A mean and mighty king of mere losers.
Make a lot of them, make them your base,
A plinth for the statue of one superstar.
They can build it and pay you with their lives.

My First Oration

Sophomore year of high school, I took Speech,
a class taught—led—by Miss Malseed
in a room with a stage called the Odeon.

Sophomore boys near year-end—and yes,
only boys—could give a memorized
oration with gestures and movement
to the Optimist Club,

a small fellowship group of businessmen,
in a room in a restaurant after dinner.
I chose democracy as my theme.

From the encyclopedia my parents bought
from a door-to-door salesman, I chose
Solon the Lawgiver of Athens and
Hiawatha, sage of the Iroquois Nation
as independent founders of democracies.

The logic of my argument from two men
out of all history now eludes me.
Feedback was that perhaps Solon was remote
and did not engage the men's interest.

From this, I learned nothing; I worked over
many years on a verse play about Solon
playing the mad poet to take power
by disrupting the women's mysteries—
my work while democracy shattered in lies.

Hiawatha's been done, but in name only,
a stolen name, not the real man.
But who knows—I might still have time
for a new draft, this time an oration
of epic ethnic appropriation.

Not a Colossus

Under circling skies, oceanside land
Cracks open, like a watershed door,
Inward, for a refugee's urgent hand,
To natural harbor, home to breathe free.

Liberty still holds up high a flame
Of green copper oxides. A few poor,
Tattered, skeletal piers remain to frame
Airy memories of a welcoming shore.

An orange obesity of fraudulent fame
Now struts and shouts to loom larger than she
Who calmly still carries Liberty's name.

The awful clown stretches to pretend to stand
Tall shakes his fists and rants at you and me,
But down he shrinks with every cruel command.

As If

As if creation lives in a better place,
above politics of crime, lies, and greed,
I resent having to vent
in verse my outrage at the disgrace
that overwhelms our news feed.

Data Mining

Data dump means data transfer,
except to experts, it's web services,
the granular scaled to enterprise expectations
as standard performance reviews scaled 1 to 4
with 2.3 the intended mean,
so harsh a feedback on daily effort,

most workers not much above the basic model
in skill set, diligence, and attendance,
dejection letters westbound
under solar plasma streaming ions
in magnetic exchange, clouded with
a confluence of energy rivers overhead and

synapse tested in an outreach customer survey.
First-quarter reports a mild end to wintry lockdowns,
accelerated take-offs in late model cars
behind engine displacement and exhaust, a car guy
on a sweet ride on an expressway, the Belt Parkway
parallel to the upper bay, as the ocean's output

hammers and erodes earthen outer works.
The sea will rise again—sailors must change
their job titles to match posted job descriptions.
Nothing to do with sails, but hardly landsmen
pressed into service, they flow in sea lanes and
coast to reach the current ends of land mass.

Continent of Fire

At plains' and prairies' end,
sharp mountains loom,
obscured by residue
of fire. Many dim gray
columns of smoke rise,
slanted like sunbeams,

reversing, it seems,
the old image of radiant grace,
a sign
to score the acrid skies.

In highland plateaus,
in desert depths,
brushfire haze
buries the mine
works that lord over days
of dry, enclosed

cities. Over many more
mountains, down
the last rounded hills to the shore,
high chaparral's left
seared beige and brown.

Evening smolders away
our power over night.
Outside our home, scorched, we wait
while losing light.

Darkening Hour

Evening, and inside
The current radiating light,
Home might yet
Waver, flicker and fade.

The hanging, shaded lamp
Sheds one large circle overhead,
A pale moon with
Edges in a penumbral blur.

The march of darkness
Has come around again
With no good answers,
Only patterns to ponder.

Light Fall

What shuttered windows will not tell
Is whether tossing thunder slept
While light cracked, shattered, and fell.

Within where children dwell,
Restless dreams like raccoons crept
Where windows will not tell.

Wake up, dear child, say all is well.
Vows of solemn silence were kept
While light cracked, shattered, and fell.

Outside are vacant homes to sell.
How hard or long the absent wept,
Shuttered windows cannot tell.

Unuttered darkness does repel
Broad vision. We must respect
The way light cracked, shattered, and fell.

Still, dreadful silence we'll dispel
And stir in the night to expect
Darker truths that windows may tell
Now that light cracked, shattered, fell.

Cry Wolf

Off-moments, all akilter,
arms akimbo, trains of
almost thoughts sliding through
when snarls of a wolf pounce

from dark edging, a sleek, grey
predator, long teeth bared.
It rips and ravages
disjoints and smears a mess

subliminal passing as sublime
glimpse of entrails
splattered on the floor.
They seem to spell wolf

but it's devoured and gone
and only I am howling.

Fear of Sleep

The least
Bit awake,
I resist

The seeping
Sweet fake
Death in sleeping.

Day's end
Is too real
A loss to feel
And pretend

Peace. But streams
Of lulling lies
Disguise
Life as dreams.

Sleeping Dragon

Steep buttes and bluffs of South China:
Fir trees atop towering cliffs,
Thin waterfall in a gap,
A gnarled pine foregrounded over
Tiny humans in ritual bowing
Outside a thatched hut:

A defeated warlord has come
With his best surviving generals
To find a reclusive scholar,
A cowherd and farmer,
The Sleeping Dragon.

The warlord needs guidance.
A Usurper, Prime Minister,
Holds the Emperor captive in his court.
The Usurper is a poet and his verses
Inspire armies. He's amassing a huge force
to cross the Yangtze River and conquer
The Southlands rich in tea and silk.

Women, uneducated, work
In crafts, in fields, at home with
Children as armies muster and swarm.
The Usurper plans to kill certain husbands
And keep two beauties in his bronze bird tower.

All the poor scholars, street
Performers, mountain hermits
And bookish cowherds
Say Sleeping Dragon is a genius

Who can perhaps outwit the Usurper.
Actually, Sleeping Dragon is second choice.
The Usurper poet has already tricked
And enslaved everyone's favorite genius.

Three times the warlord comes
To an isolated, thatched hut.
Each time a different riffraff
Scholar says the Dragon is not home.

Oh, he went for a walk, I guess,
Might be gone for days. Yes,
These are his books and lute.
You can stay if you like, but
He might be visiting friends or
Off on a journey by boat to old books.

His generals recoil in outrage, but
The warlord, desperate uncle
Of the helpless Prince, bows and waits.

Sleeping Dragon returns from the hills.
He holds as his own the fanciful
Folklore name for this rugged ridge.

Foresight flares
From the Dragon's mouth—
Fire will be their fiercest weapon!

Our Song

Ah, memories of the day's outrages
Cut sharply as we fade into sleep.
What we leave behind still matters.
We can't escape a world so strange.

We sing like a rebel army marching
Through a village to sirens and applause.
I grind my teeth. You stir and toss.
We murder our fathers with loud guitars.

We awaken again to what's been lost
And clamor in darkness for a past
Before the fascists came, reclaimed.

Please strum your banjo. I'll string a fiddle.
The tune evolves, a tender call together
To start a day again, in the right key.

By All His Engins

A New Day

So bright day is back:
Weather mild, sky open,
Crowds welcoming and brisk.

Civic Center buildings shine
Through tree branches
Still bare in City Hall Park.

I walk just far enough
From work at lunch to reach
A Japanese bakery and savor

A bowl of pale green bean soup.

Gowanus

These blocks to the west, Gowanus,
Feel all at once familiar: brick & cement
Sheds for industry and warehousing,
One to three stories high.
The grid of streets looks largely abandoned.
From shoulder to shoulder, all is sky.

I could muse in solitude here
As I lived for years a few miles north,
Just north of the mouth of Newtown Creek,
Another waterway dredged from a stream.
Years of bounty: surround me again,
Pacing through mills by rivers to find work.

Here, the Canal is narrow and brackish,
Smelling of long-stagnant water over murk.
We once rowed a canoe around a bend
Into the main channel, wide and high-walled
By vast machines, a crushing scale upon us,
Suddenly too close to home, Gowanus.

Painted yellow, a taxi fleet garage bustles
By yellow cabs through two doors, the curb lined,
Interior deep with cabs. Nearby, THE NEWS
Brooklyn Garage is a faded expanse.
(80,000 square feet will divide).
Around the corner is an open door, inside . . .

People, active, artists? A big bright project
Consumes them. It's another fun house,
A rock-climbing place with colorful cliffs.
Dozens of fit young people scale the walls
Or cluster merrily below. More and more
Arrive behind me, flowing in as I recede.

These streets are more than a ghosted work zone,
A site to mourn the truckers of yore
And the nightly dispatch of dirty newsprint.
The City awakes, still young and moving in.
Up the block, people throng a new bar
Where the back room has a stage, shows films

Of climbing mountains, an enthusiasm.
A stage—poets and dreamers, alert!
This close to home, fresh life is a flirt.

When Here

When here, I am my ancestor.
On the same dark street, he hurries
Past distant storefronts glowing green,
Keeps looking ahead to find me.

That guy was a curb-sitter,
A brick front, a pacing train chaser.
Night was summer's wild time, cooler

And still open late as we emerge
Bright-eyed from desert nests under
Prickly-pear cactus, teddy-bear choyo,
From holes. Tribal lore is still expressed

As mysteries: what makes this,
What am I to it?
But still, in the night, it stirs and strikes.

Resolution

Please tell me why
the sun withdraws
its claim each night
and serves again at dawn.

You know the stars will try
to answer late. They'll light
up changing, restless laws
of loss within what's won.

The calendar each day
rules matters will continue.
The parties will go on.

I love how you can stay
well-grounded till our work is done:
Disputes resolve within you.

Our Real Estate

Séance sayonara, O ghost of dreams!
Levitate above long confidence schemes.

Few cowboys ever owned a ranch.
Alien cattle munch scrub grass down to dust.

What dudes we are, masters of land
Local and sublime, how fortunate

A real
       estate we pass through—
Human bonds that promise tomorrow.

A Moth

This glow is inviting.
Flitter closer. It warms,
Enlightens and reveals you.
Circle and float, bask and enjoy—
If it gets too hot, back off.

Now you know
Your safe distance through
Enlivening experience.
You love this loving warmth.
You can safely return.

You are this feeling of
Being drawn into Beauty
Beyond and becoming you.
Dance around your fire.
Dare to dive!

Feel the burn!

V

Bread bakers,
bed breakers,

shocked in the **V**
of a bed just broken,
in close embrace agree,
though only laughter's spoken:
        Fallen so low!

The mattress may be steep,
but squeezed together so,
On we go!
On we go!
        And drop into sleep.

From the Stars

Electrons dance into
new clusters.
Charges mate in
magnetic moments,
fuse bonds, release
radiant energy

Explode!
Supernova expels
iron, silver, gold, zinc,
rare minerals
seeding the next world.

Fresh water brims ponds.
Let there be plenty,
tending fields here, unafraid.

Live as a Poet by Example
to Create a New World

Can an old man live a new way,
become a new man of the next age,
an example and change agent,
a guide to self-discovery
and fundamental change?
Perhaps through making humorous
quips and eccentric puzzles?

That sounds like ego whimsy, strutting
all dressed-up in youthful foppery,
red, curly-toed shoes,
hair dyed black; belly corseted tight,
gleefully rushing to rendezvous with . . .

   . . . not the luring seductress,
but robbers who beat and strip him,
leave him to the kicks and mockery
of all his neighbors.
What an amusing end to
Psyche's dream magic!

No, that won't do. That's a farce,
not poetry.

   Instead, perhaps,
just cook meals, do the laundry
—Yes, that's it—
do the househusband work
and be proud. Serve a plate
of roasted greens and seared salmon.

One Plus One

Tango passion, hambone hip, I vote for you.
You peel me open to air out fresh nutrients
And sear them in a large, ovenproof pan.
You pour me into your pie of the day.

Enjoy whatever you might find to like in me.
Others have and have moved on. Their hunger
Lingers and burns through nights as I sweat.
How pale I was as one of two and then two others.

Now I come up with the sun in sober arrogance,
All shining and smiling like a just world,
With jokes and joys to share over time.

Now we are one and can see through our clothes.
Comic book ads for x-ray glasses have nothing on us,
As solid in our solitude as sated panthers.

Bloom

In the short time we have, we have
to nod to cold winds, sway
and bend in storms, soak
up what falls.

Still, we hold firm in the earth
grow, unfurl, open.

Sunday, March 15, 2020

Bright day at the
Brooklyn Botanic Garden
to see magnolias bloom
while I can. And they are
coming into full bloom,
creamy yellow bulbs,
white stars bursting open,
as are a hillside of daffodils.

A big surprise is one cherry tree
in bold pink blossom,
while all around it,
others sprout just tight dark buds
on bare branches. This look,
this good long walk will have to do
for weeks, months, or more
as we shelter-in-place

in deadly pandemic quarantine.
Immune, flowers will flourish unseen.

Together Daily

Together daily, we've sipped then drunk love's
Refreshing ecstasies like caffeinated
Green tea. We nestle, paired, ceramic doves
(Once all aflutter, till storms abated).

Wrapped in comforts, how big we become.
Cruel time, while leaving, still holds us here,
Embracing our time together. We're from
The future, savoring now what stays dear.

Under Venus, surer than night's brightest star,
We each take our turn at the wheel
On the highway in a fast-moving car,
Floor the gas and speed with spirit and zeal.

Our high beams pierce the darkening road.
We're headed where even mountains erode.

Sunday, March 14, 2021

Confined a year in a deadly pandemic,
Emerging from a cold, snowbound winter
Into brilliant sunlight, a steady wind,
I've reserved a socially distanced walk
In the Brooklyn Botanic Garden.

February's lasting snowstorm slowed the spring.
No cherry tree blooms early this year.
Magnolia buds seem mere pussy willows.
Daffodil Hill has only sheaves of leaves,
Tipped with yellow daubs if you look closely.

But oh, crocus blooms in abundance,
Blanketing the berm abutting Flatbush
Avenue. Orange-tongued, purple, ground cover
Crocus is no solitary venture
Out into life. It's nestled, teeming crowds!

Chasms

Sullen gulleys cleave the swollen hills and
Gorge in water, drain and sink through dark soil,
Twist through sundered rockface as slinking streams.

In summer's hot rain, winds of change boil
And evaporate, dissolving airborne.
The world is no longer what it seems

In sunny days and dreams. Our promised land
Has been exhausted by its people, torn.
What trickles down will find new depths.

Ironworker

Clubfooted worker drone, Vulcan of fires,
Volcano spewing fumes, forge of flames,
Blacksmith, smithy of blades and axe heads,
Armor-maker, breastplate and greaves, shields
For flesh that, sliced, splits, spills, and empties,

Outcast, deformed, with chunks of meteor
Or outcroppings of ore, discolored rocks
To heat and beat, smash into tools, despised
Triumphant drunk, riding a mule to the gods
To shape good uses out of studied ground

Dug, burnt, beaten, sweated, toiled, struck
With ringing resonance, clang of impure to
Power taking form, horseshoes for war steeds,
Weapons for warlords and dim wannabes,
Hammered on the anvil, bellowing hot air.

Empedocles at Geysir

In Iceland, hot springs are so pervasive,
Many workers plunge into them at lunchtime
With their colleagues. Great Geysir is inland
On a narrow road. There, strong winds keep
Blustering. Keep children in the car.

There I read that nineteenth-century tourists
Threw rocks down its well, hoping to see
The waterspout blast the rocks high skyward
When it erupts, soars. Their rocks block Geysir—
Or fewer strong earthquakes calms it for now.

As I stare down into the rock-rimmed ruin,
At the entombed, crushed waste of a wonder,
Sudden gusting winds shove and propel me
Teetering, all but throw me, fast, off the
Cliff of earth's charred, hardened crust, down, down . . .

What a Sun God Sees

The Sun sees more than light, sees
All it feels and frees, constantly
Becoming primal turmoil
In mass ejections of ion waves
On outreach vectors far into nothing.

Within its plasma's twisting grasp,
Metal and gas globes always shine, exposed.
Planets flit like gravity-trapped gnats,
Adrift in solar wind. A few wear glitter.
The Sun's charged dust streams past them

Like comet tails and dances in aurora crowns.
Milky skim half-covers a deep blue stone,
A swirly with green and brown
Trace elements. It rotates under
Vapors that veil lands and seas.

When clouds wide as continents pass on,
Drylands lay bare and beige,
A scorched mirror reflecting
Solar turbulence, flares, and storms
As an inert wash of one glaring color.

Under crumpled mountains
In parallel ranks, deserts cook
A cream soup with spillage unstirred,
Soured curds and whey, baked scum
As overdone Sun, an old offering.

But the Sun God sees no night, not one glimpse
Of cities lit in darkness, in cellular
Patterns of nodes and neuron pathways,
Never where we settle and shine with our backs
Turned, spinning our own ways beyond Him.

Yet ultimate electromagnetic
Power is His. From every neon
And fluorescent night, we soon return,
Impelled to face Him
Where He writhes and pulses, unrelenting.

End Notes

The section headings are phrases from John Milton's *Paradise Lost,* Book I, lines 562, 673, 674, 701, and 750.

In "Wallace Stevens Loses His Job," certain details are from *Parts of A World: Wallace Stevens Remembered,* by Peter Brazeau.

In "Marcy," the quotation and certain details are from *Northern Men with Southern Loyalties: The Democratic Party and the Sectional Crisis,* by Michael Todd Landis.

"Sleeping Dragon" describes the artwork *Visiting the Thatched Hut Three Times* by Dai Jin and aspects of the ancient epic novel *Romance of the Three Kingdoms.*

About the Author

William Considine was born in McKeesport, PA. Attending on work-study, loans and scholarships, he graduated "With Great Distinction" from Stanford and *cum laude* from Harvard Law School.

He writes poems and plays. Fast Speaking Music released a CD of his poems with music, *An Early Spring* (2013). The Operating System published a chapbook of poems, *Strange Coherence* (2013) and a volume of his early, produced verse plays, *The Furies* (2017). Finishing Line Press published a poetry chapbook, *The Other Myrtle* (2021).

His full-length play *Moral Support* ran at Medicine Show Theatre, NYC in 2019. to critical praise. His full-length verse play *Women's Mysteries* had a staged reading at Polaris North, NYC in 2019. His latest short verse plays seen in New York City in 2020—2021 include Aunt Peg and the Comptometer, Persephone's Return, Odyssey's End, John Milton in the Tower, and A Common Tongue.

He lives with his wife in Brooklyn, NY. They have two grown daughters. A retired lawyer, he is a member of The Dramatists Guild, Polaris North theater artists cooperative and Brevitas, a poet's cooperative.

(williamconsidine.com)

www.ingramcontent.com/pod-product-compliance
Lightning Source LLC
Chambersburg PA
CBHW070548090426
42735CB00013B/3111